Read for a Better World™

PARASAUROLOPHUS

A First Look

TOM JACKSON

Lerner Publications ◆ Minneapolis

Educator Toolbox

Reading books is a great way for kids to express what they're interested in. Before reading this title, ask the reader these questions:

What do you think this book is about? Look at the cover for clues.

What do you already know about this dinosaur?

What do you want to learn about this dinosaur?

Let's Read Together

Encourage the reader to use the pictures to understand the text.

Point out when the reader successfully sounds out a word.

Praise the reader for recognizing sight words such as *the* and *it*.

TABLE OF CONTENTS

Parasaurolophus

Parasaurolophus was a type of dinosaur. It lived seventy-five million years ago.

Parasaurolophus
PAH-ruh-saw-ROL-uh-fuhs

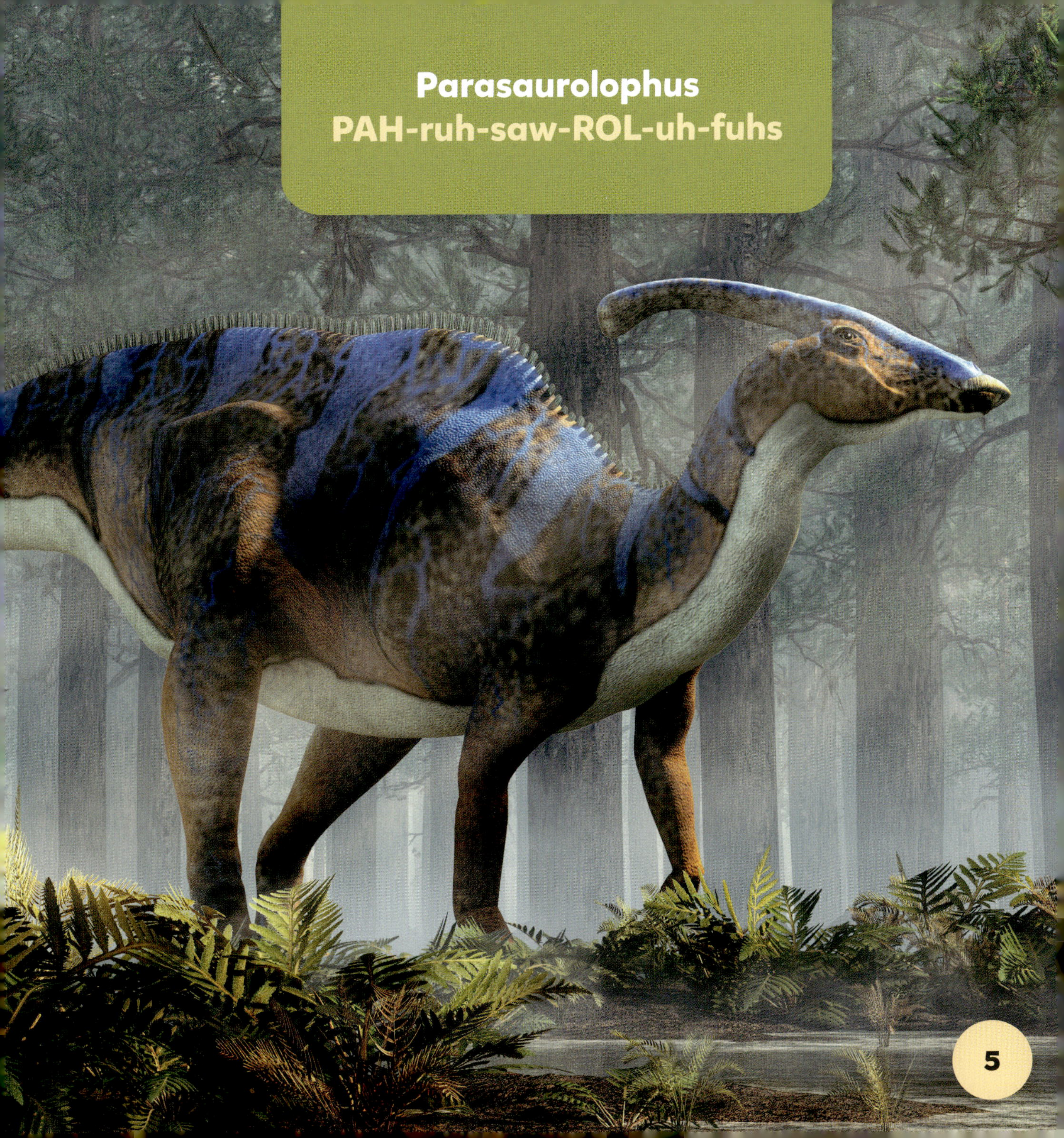

Its mouth looked like
a duck's bill.

The dinosaur had a
tall crest on its head.

The crest might have been brightly colored.

The dinosaur might have used its crest to make louder calls.

What else could the crest have been used for?

The dinosaur was as long as a school bus.

What other animals are long?

The dinosaur had four legs.

It could stand up on
its back two legs.

The dinosaur had many small teeth. It ate leaves and pine needles.

What other animals have small teeth?

The dinosaur is
not alive today.
But people
find its bones.

The bones teach us
about the dinosaur.

You Connect!

What is something you like about this dinosaur?

What else is as big as this dinosaur?

What other dinosaurs do you know about?

STEM Snapshot

Encourage students to think and ask questions like scientists. Ask the reader:

What is something you learned about this dinosaur?

What is something you noticed in the pictures of the dinosaur?

What is something you still don't know about this dinosaur?

Photo Glossary

bone

crest

duckbill

leaves

Learn More

Greve, Meg, *Super-Incredible Dinosaurs*. Mankato, MN: Black Rabbit Books, 2025.

Hansen, Grace. *Parasaurolophus*. Minneapolis: Abdo Kids Jumbo, 2020.

Hulick, Kathryn. *Dinosaurs*. Minneapolis: Abdo Reference, 2023.

Index

Photo Acknowledgments

The images in this book are used with the permission of: © Daniel Eskridge/Shutterstock Images, pp. 5, 10–11; © Dotted Yeti/Shutterstock Images, pp. 6, 9, 14, 16–17, 23 (duckbill), 23 (leaves); © WhirlVFX - Pamela Werrell/Shutterstock Images, p. 7; © Warpaint/Shutterstock Images, p. 8; © Kostiantyn Ivanyshen/Shutterstock Images, p. 12–13; © Louiss Aude/Shutterstock Images, pp. 12–13; © Mark Turner/Dreamstime.com, p. 15, 23 (crest); © AKKHARAT JARUSILAWONG/Shutterstock Images, pp. 18, 23 (bone); © Matthew Dicker/Shutterstock Images, p. 20.

Cover Photograph: © Daniel Eskridge/Shutterstock Images

Design Elements: © Mighty Media, Inc.

Lerner Publications Company
An imprint of Lerner Publishing Group, Inc.
241 First Avenue North
Minneapolis, MN 55401 USA

For reading levels and more information, look up this title at www.lernerbooks.com.

Main body text set in Mikado a Medium.
Typeface provided by Hannes von Doehren.

Library of Congress Cataloging-in-Publication Data

Names: Jackson, Tom, 1972-author
Title: Parasaurolophus : a first look / Tom Jackson.
Description: Minneapolis : Lerner Publications, [2026] | Series: Read about dinosaurs : read for a better world | Includes bibliographical references and index. | Audience: Ages 5–8 | Audience: Grades K–1 | Summary: "The Parasaurolophus was an interesting, duckbilled dinosaur. Parts of this dino are still a mystery. But with photorealistic images and informational text, readers can see what scientists think about this prehistoric creature"—Provided by publisher.
Identifiers: LCCN 2025011288 (print) | LCCN 2025011289 (ebook) | ISBN 9798765689806 lib. bdg. | ISBN 9798348029067 pbk | ISBN 9798765697665 epub
Subjects: LCSH: Parasaurolophus—Juvenile literature
Classification: LCC QE862.O65 J294 2026 (print) | LCC QE862.O65 (ebook) | DDC 567.914—dc23/eng/20250614

LC record available at https://lccn.loc.gov/2025011288
LC ebook record available at https://lccn.loc.gov/2025011289

Manufactured in the United States of America
1 - CG - 12/15/25